# —SCIENCE—
## THROUGH THE
# —SEASONS—

# AUTUMN
# IN THE WOOD

# —SCIENCE— THROUGH THE —SEASONS—

# AUTUMN IN THE WOOD

## Janet Fitzgerald

Hamish Hamilton · London

*Acknowledgement*

I should like to express my gratitude to the schools, teachers and children with whom I have worked, and with whose help I have gained the experience and confidence needed to write this series. I am particularly indebted to those schools which allowed photographs to be taken as the children carried out their investigations. Thanks are also due to Chris Fairclough for some of the excellent photographs illustrating the texts. Finally, I am most grateful to my editors, Anna Sandeman and Sue Twiselton, for all their encouragement and professional advice.

*Janet Fitzgerald*

The author and publisher would also like to thank the following for permission to reproduce photographs: Heather Angel cover (right), pages 7, 11, 23; ARDEA pages 18, 24, 25; Chris Fairclough cover (left), pages 6, 8, 9, 12, 13, 14, 15, 17, 19, 20, 21; NHPA pages 10, 22; OSF Picture Library page 16.

First published in Great Britain 1987 by
Hamish Hamilton Children's Books
27 Wrights Lane, London W8 5TZ
Copyright © 1987 by Janet Fitzgerald

British Library Cataloguing in Publication Data
Fitzgerald, Janet
Autumn in the wood. – (Science through
the seasons).
1. Autumn – Juvenile literature
I. Title   II. Series
574.5′43        QH81
ISBN 0–241–12093–4

Printed in Great Britain by
William Clowes Ltd, Beccles, Suffolk

# Author's note

Books in this series are intended for use by young children actively engaged in exploring the environment in the company of a teacher or parent. Many lifelong interests are formed at this early age, and a caring attitude towards plants, animals and resources can be nurtured to become a mature concern for conservation in general.

The basis for all scientific investigation rests on the ability to observe closely and to ask questions. These books aim to increase a child's awareness so that he or she learns to make accurate observations. First-hand experience is encouraged and simple investigations of observations are suggested. The child will suggest many more! The aim is to give children a broad base of experience and 'memories' on which to build for the future.

# Contents

# It is Autumn in the wood and the leaves are changing colou

What colours can you see?

What is changing colour in the wood?

What will happen to the leaves?

Collect some coloured leaves.

Look at one leaf.

Is there a brown part?

Where is the brown part?

Are there other colours in your leaf?

Where are the other colours?

# It is Autumn in the wood and
## rain falls on the leaves

What shape are the raindrops?

Will the rain stay on the leaves?

What will happen to the rain?

Use a watering can
to water plants and
bushes outside.

Watch how the water
rolls off the leaves.

Does any water
stay on?

Watch to see where
most of the water goes.

# It is Autumn in the wood and
## leaves fall from the trees

Are all the leaves on the ground?

Where have most of the leaves
collected?

What will happen to the leaves
on the ground?

Find a tree and look closely at
the leaves underneath it.

Has anything happened to their
shape?

Walk in the leaves and listen
to the sound they make.

# It is Autumn in the wood and
## you may find some blackberrie

Which blackberries are ripe?

You can eat blackberries if they are ripe.

Birds like to eat blackberries, too.

Pick some blackberries.

Look at the place where the blackberries grow.

Look at their leaves and stem.

Look carefully at one blackberry.

Do you know any other fruits which look like this?

It is Autumn in the wood and
we can collect winged seeds
from the sycamore tree.

Why do the seeds have wings?

What will happen to them when
the wind blows?

Collect some winged seeds from a sycamore tree.

Make your seeds fly.

Is it best to throw them into the air?

What happens if you drop them?

Do they always land in the same place?

**It is Autumn in the wood and**
**cones fall to the groun**

Cones carry the seeds of a tree.

Look at the shape of the cones.

Where will the cones land when they fall from the tree?

Will the cones roll away?

Try to find some other kinds of cone.

You may have to visit other areas of woodland to do this.

Sort the cones.

Are they the same size?

Are they all the same shape and colour?

How are they different?

# It is Autumn in the wood and
## birds and other animals eat berrie

What colour are the berries?

How does the colour help the bird
to find the berries?

Why does the bird collect berries?

Pick some different kinds of berries.

DANGER Berries must *not* be eaten.

Are all the berries the same colour?

What shapes are the berries?

How are they growing on the stem?

Hang your berries outside.

Watch to see if the birds eat them.

# It is Autumn in the wood and fungi can be foun[d]

Where are the fungi growing?

Are the fungi easy to see?

Fungi grow in many different places in a wood.

DANGER  Most fungi must *not* be eaten.

Ask an adult to help you find or buy a mushroom.

A mushroom is a type of fungus.

Feel the top of the mushroom.

Feel underneath the mushroom.

What does the stalk look like?

Draw the mushroom, showing all its parts.

# It is Autumn in the wood and
## there is mist among the trees

What does the mist look like?

Mist often feels damp and soft.

When it is misty, spiders' webs can be seen clearly.

Try to find a spider's web and look at the spider.

Be careful not to harm it.

How many legs has the spider got?

How many parts has its body got?

Draw a picture of the spider's web.

## It is Autumn in the wood and small animals move in the leaves

This vole is looking for food.

How does it find its food?

What do voles like to eat?

Can you find out?

Collect some nuts and other seeds
from trees and plants.

If you have a hamster or gerbil
watch how it eats a nut or seed.

How does it hold the nut or seed?

Look at the shape of the nuts and seeds.

Does the shape help the animal to feed?

# For teachers and parents

We all recognise that children possess an insatiable curiosity about the rich environment and exciting experiences around them. For this reason they have a natural affinity for science and a basic inclination to explore and discover the world in which we live. We need to foster this sense of wonder by encouraging a scientific way of thinking in the early years. Children's own experience of the immediate environment will provide a natural starting point.

Through science children can evolve an active process of enquiry. This begins with observation (including sorting, comparing, ordering and measuring) and continues with asking questions, devising practical investigations, predicting outcomes, controlling variables, noting results, and perhaps modifying the original question in the light of discovery. The books in this series offer suggestions for engaging young children in this sort of active enquiry by relating seasonal change to familiar surroundings.

## Extension activities

### pp. 6–7

Encourage children to observe and investigate trees at home, in the garden, on the way to school, and in the school grounds. Notice how leaves change colour, and which colours they change to. Check which trees begin to change colour first, and which leaves change first. If all the lower leaves change colour first, are these the first to fall?

### pp. 8–9

Children love rain, and investigations involving water and puddles are carried out with enthusiasm. Children might observe where water collects, how quickly it soaks away or evaporates, and what is left behind.

The shape of raindrops and condensation can be discussed. Collecting rain in a home-made container, and recording different amounts of rainwater, leads to questions about the rainiest days, weeks, or months. It can also be related to tree and plant growth.

Trees and leaves with inadequate moisture provide another topic. What happens to plants during spells of dry weather? Look at damp places around the school or in the garden. What plants grow there? How do they differ from those growing in dry places?

**pp. 10–11**

Investigate the patterns of leaf fall. Which trees lose their leaves first? Is the position of the tree important? Which leaves fall first? Relate the fall to leaf opening in Spring. Observe leaves falling from one tree. How far away do the leaves fall? How does leaf fall differ on a still day and on a windy day?

**pp. 12–13**

If possible, go out blackberry-picking. Help the children to see that the bramble is a climbing plant, and look for other climbers to compare it with. Try cooking with the fruit – making jams, jellies and pies etc. Use the juice as dye for wool or tie-and-dye fabric.

**pp. 14–15**

Compare the flight patterns of tree seeds. Does the double sycamore key perform better than the single ash? What happens if you remove one of the sycamore wings? Visit a tree standing on its own and look at the seed distribution around it. The tree could be in your garden or school grounds. How far away do the seeds fall? Look for evidence of seedlings nearby. Plant some of the seeds.

**pp. 16–17**

Many sorting, comparing and weighing activities are possible with cones. Observe the regular patterns on the outside of cones. Are they the same on all cones?

Place a cone in water for 1 day/week. Observe the change in shape, and measure the weight before and after immersion. How long does it take for the cone to dry out again?

Look at a branch with cones attached and see where they are growing. Look underneath a tree to see where the cones fall. Does the shape of the cone help with the distribution of the seeds? Investigate this by rolling, dropping and throwing the cone. Do the seeds fall out? Plant some of the seeds.

**pp. 18–19**

Winter feeding and hibernation can be discussed. Is the wood a good place for finding and storing food, and for building up reserves of energy before the Winter? Observe the difference between berries: whether they grow in bunches, or singly; and how they are attached to a twig. Count the number of berries in a bunch of hawthorn or rowan. Is there an average? Look inside the berry at the seeds. How many seeds are there? How thick is the berry's skin? Emphasise very firmly that no berries should be eaten.

## pp. 20–21

There are some interesting and lovely fungi in woods, which children find fascinating. If accompanied by an adult, who can point out the dangers and supervise hand-washing afterwards, some investigations can be carried out.

Notice the colours of the fungi, and the places in which they are found. Introduce the topic of camouflage in nature, noticing in particular the fungi's colours, textures and shapes, and how well they blend into woodland.

Look for fungi on the playing fields at school or on the lawn at home. Notice the distribution and patterns of growth. Watch a clump of fungi develop over a few days. What happens when the fungi begin to fade? Choose one large cap and place it, gills down, on a sheet of white paper overnight. With luck, you should have a spore print. Spray gently with hair lacquer to stop it fading away.

## pp. 22–23

Spiders' webs have different patterns, e.g. wheel webs, cobwebs, hammock or tangled webs. Where is each kind of web found most often? Can you suggest reasons for this? Find out which kind of web is most common in your garden or school grounds. Study any remains of food in a web and decide which sort of food the spider likes best. Look for the discarded skins of spiders.

## pp. 24–25

It is unlikely that children will be able to see the small mammals which live in a wood, so good pictures and photographs are essential. Comparisons can be made with animals they already know, such a hamsters, gerbils, rabbits and guinea pigs. Do they eat different foods? Are they different in size? Look at the legs and feet, and the shape of head, whisker and eyes. Is a wood a good place for a small mammal to live?

# Index